The Underground Railroad

by Margaret McNamara

Table of Contents

Introduction	2
Chapter 1 What Was Slavery?	4
Chapter 2 What Was the Underground Railroad?	10
Chapter 3 Who Was Harriet Tubman?	18
Chapter 4 Why Was the Underground Railroad Important?	22
Summary	28
Glossary	30
Index	32

Introduction

The United States had **slavery** long ago. The **slaves** wanted to **escape**. Slaves used the **Underground Railroad** to escape.

▲ Slaves wanted to escape.

Read to learn about slavery. Read to learn about the Underground Railroad.

Words to Know

 abolitionists

 escape

 Harriet Tubman

 law

 routes

 slavery

 slaves

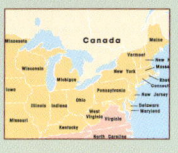 the North

 the South

 Underground Railroad

See the Glossary on page 30.

Chapter 1

What Was Slavery?

Slavery was people owning other people. The United States had slavery long ago. People brought slaves from Africa at first. Then slaves were born in the United States.

It's a Fact
The United States had slavery before the Civil War.

▲ People brought the slaves on ships.

Some slaves lived in **the North**. Most slaves lived in **the South**.

Some people in the South owned plantations. Plantations were large farms. Many slaves worked on the plantations.

The North and the South

Chapter 1

Many slaves planted crops on the plantations. The slaves picked the crops.

▲ Slaves planted crops.

Some slaves worked in big houses. The big houses were on the plantations.

▲ Some slaves worked in big houses.

It's a Fact

Crops grew on plantations. Some crops were cotton. Some crops were rice. Some crops were tobacco.

What Was Slavery?

Slaves did not earn money. Many slaves lived in small houses. The houses were cabins. Many slaves lived in each cabin.

▲ Slaves lived in this cabin.

Chapter 1

People did not let slaves learn to read. People did not let slaves own land. People did not let slaves own houses.

The United States, Mexico, and Canada

What Was Slavery?

The slaves wanted to be free. These slaves wanted to escape. These slaves wanted to leave the South. Many slaves wanted to go to the North. Many slaves wanted to go to Canada. Many slaves wanted to go to Mexico.

Chapter 2

What Was the Underground Railroad?

The Underground Railroad was a way to freedom. The Underground Railroad **routes** went from the South. Many routes went to the North. Some routes went to Canada. Some routes went to Mexico. Slaves used the routes to escape.

Routes of the Underground Railroad

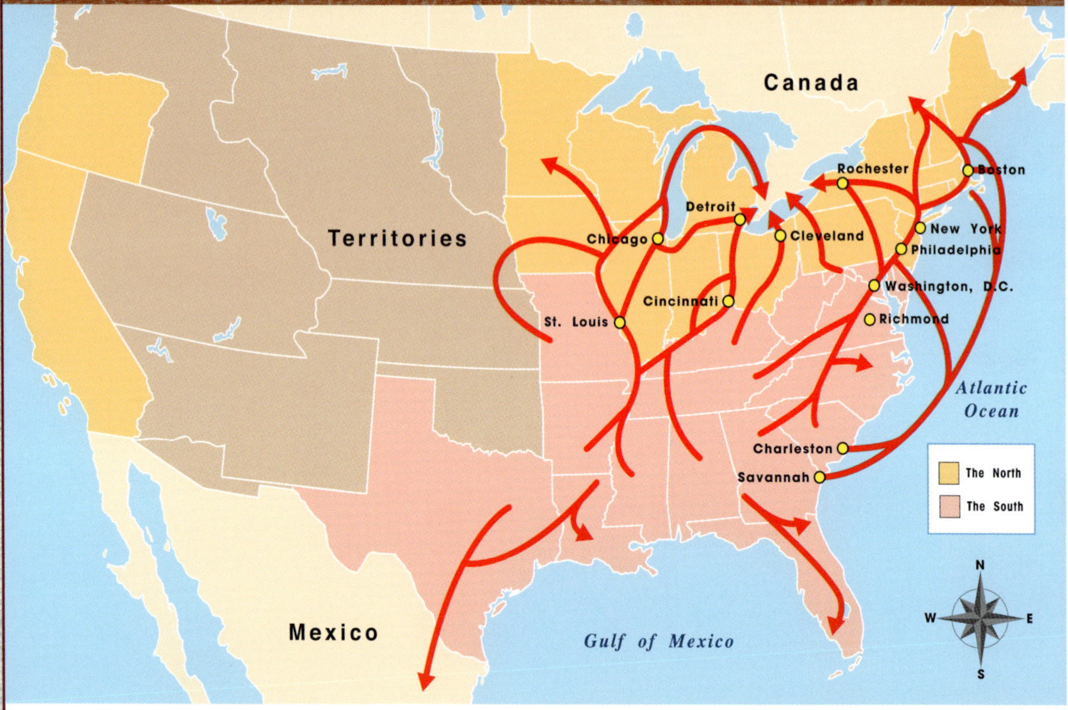

Did You Know?
The Underground Railroad was not really a railroad. The Underground Railroad was a way to escape.

The Underground Railroad was a group of people. The people were **abolitionists**. Abolitionists thought slavery was wrong. Abolitionists helped the slaves to escape.

▲ Abolitionists helped the slaves.

Did You Know?
The Underground Railroad was not really underground. Underground can mean secret. The Underground Railroad was a secret way to freedom.

Chapter 2

Some abolitionists showed slaves the routes. The slaves followed the routes. The slaves often walked. The slaves often traveled in boats. The slaves often traveled at night.

Picture This

Look at the art on pages 12–13. Pretend you are an abolitionist. How do you help the slaves?

▲ Slaves followed the routes at night.

What Was the Underground Railroad?

Many slaves looked at the North Star. The North Star was in the sky. The North Star showed the way north.

Did You Know?

Slaves followed the Drinking Gourd in the sky. The Drinking Gourd was the Big Dipper. The Big Dipper was a group of stars. The Big Dipper pointed to the North Star.

▲ Slaves looked at the stars.

Figure It Out

Why did slaves travel at night?

Chapter 2

The slaves traveled many miles. Some slaves traveled hundreds of miles. The slaves rested at safe houses.

Abolitionists owned the safe houses. Abolitionists gave food to the slaves. Abolitionists gave clothing to the slaves.

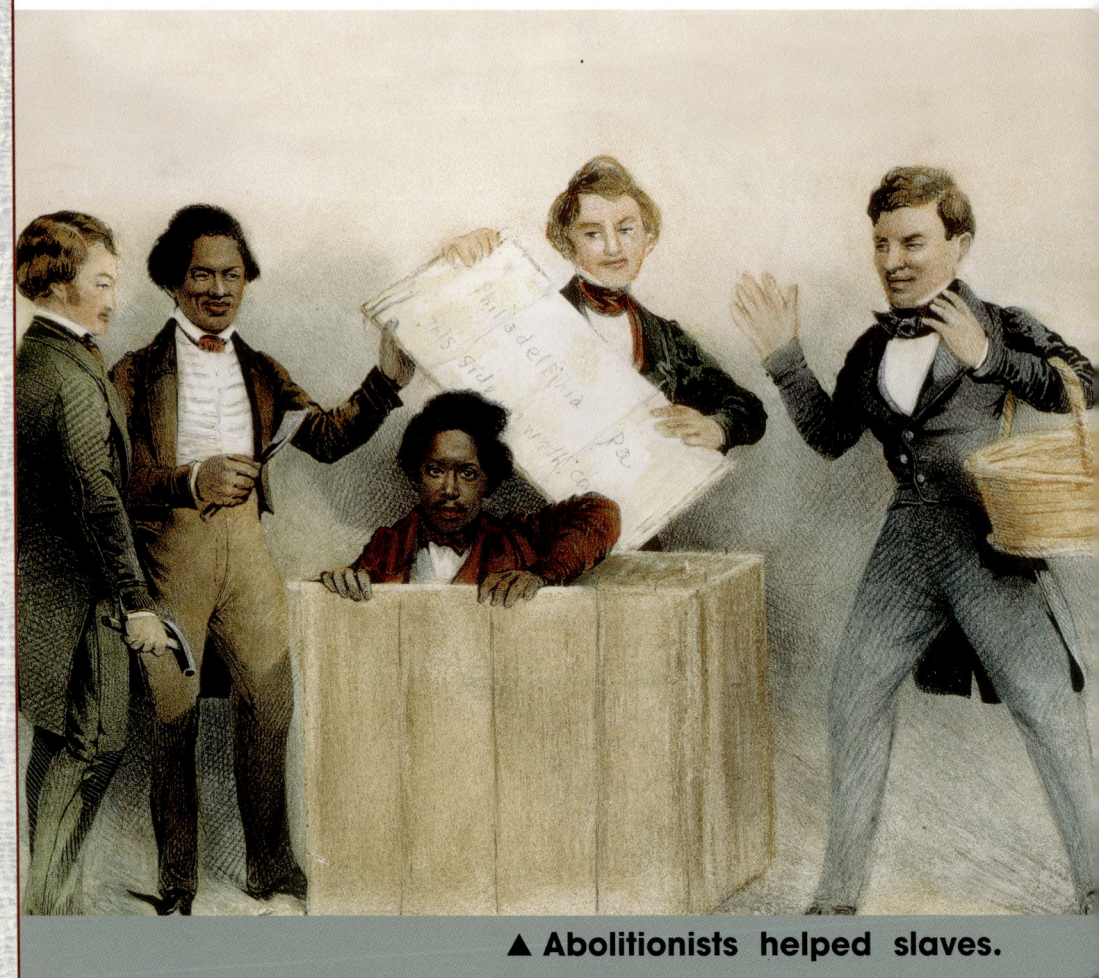

▲ Abolitionists helped slaves.

What Was the Underground Railroad?

Many abolitionists were African Americans. Many abolitionists were Quakers.

Famous Abolitionists

▲ Frederick Douglass was a slave. Then Douglass became free. Douglass helped slaves to escape. He gave speeches against slavery.

▲ Levi Coffin was a Quaker. The Quakers believed slavery was wrong. Coffin helped more than 2,000 slaves escape.

Chapter 2

People used special words for the Underground Railroad. The chart shows some of the words. The chart shows what the words mean.

Words for the Underground Railroad

Word	What the Word Means
conductors	people who helped slaves find the routes
passengers	the slaves
railroad	1. routes for slaves to follow 2. abolitionists who helped the slaves escape
stations	safe houses where slaves rested

What Was the Underground Railroad?

Chapter 3

Who Was Harriet Tubman?

Harriet Tubman was a famous abolitionist. Tubman was a conductor on the Underground Railroad. Tubman helped slaves to escape.

▲ Harriet Tubman

Harriet Tubman was born in Maryland. Tubman was a slave. Tubman worked very hard.

Did You Know?

Maryland was in the South.

Maryland
Atlantic Ocean
N
W
E
S

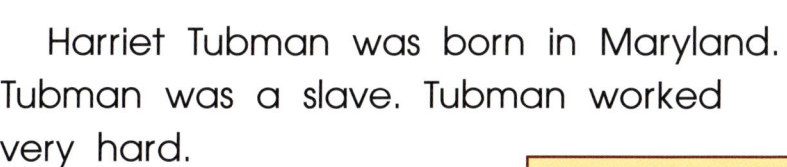

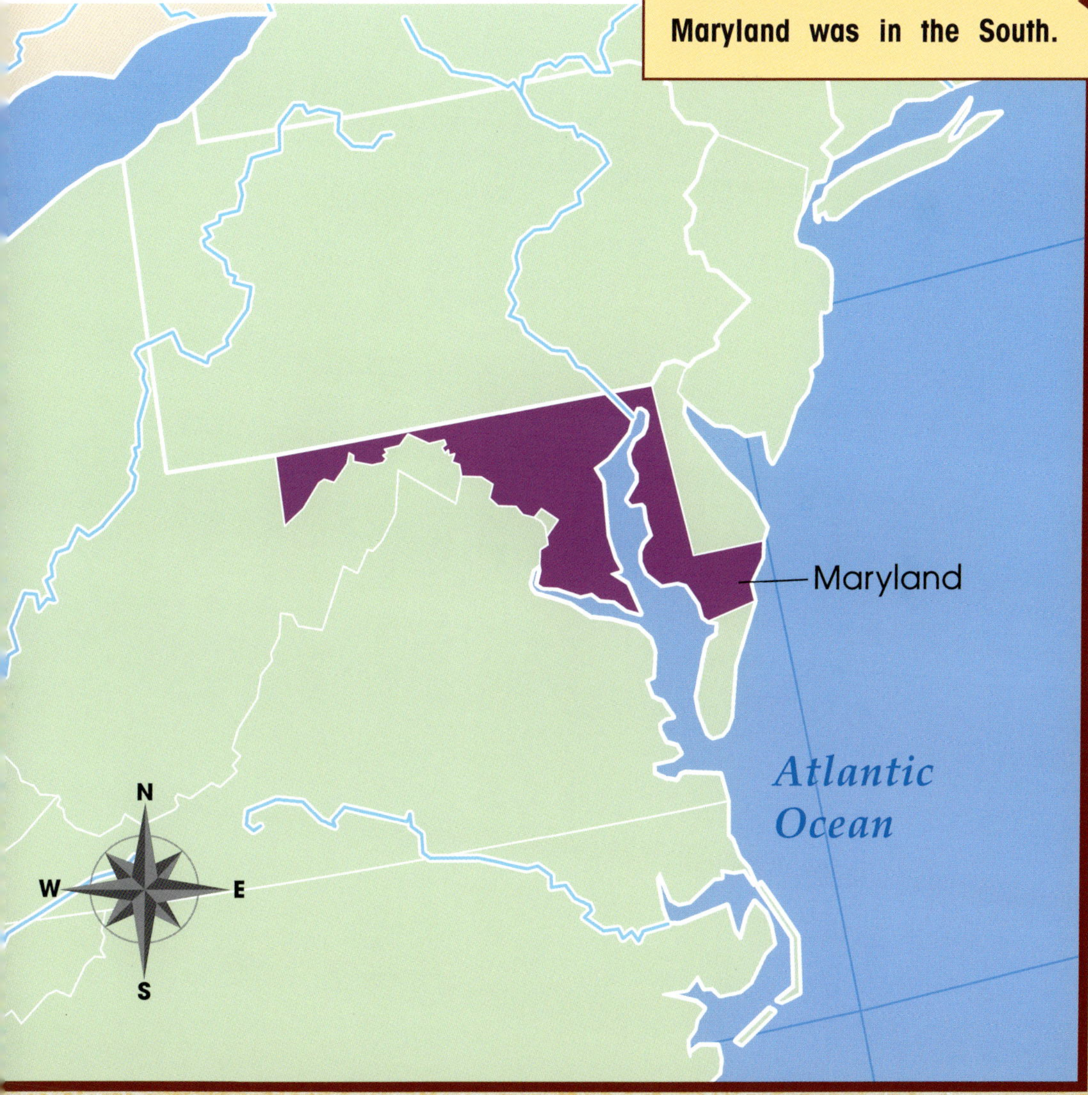

Chapter 3

Tubman wanted to be free. Conductors on the Underground Railroad helped Tubman escape. Harriet Tubman went to the North. Tubman went to Pennsylvania.

▲ Tubman escaped to Philadelphia.

Who Was Harriet Tubman?

Tubman became a conductor on the Underground Railroad. Harriet Tubman showed many slaves the routes. Harriet Tubman helped the slaves escape. She helped more than 300 slaves escape. She helped her family escape.

▲ Harriet Tubman

▲ Harriet Tubman helped slaves.

Solve This

Harriet Tubman was born about 1820. Tubman died in 1913. About how many years did Harriet Tubman live?

Answer: about 93 years

Chapter 4

Why Was the Underground Railroad Important?

Thousands of slaves used the Underground Railroad. Thousands of slaves escaped. Some slaves escaped to the North. Some slaves escaped to Canada. Some slaves escaped to Mexico.

Picture This

Look at the art on page 22. Pretend you escaped the South. What will your new life be like?

▲ Slaves used the Underground Railroad to escape.

The South was angry about the slaves. Some Southern people wanted the slaves. Some Southern people wanted a **law**. The law was about slaves. The law said the slaves must return.

▲ This law said slaves must return.

It's a Fact

The law was the Fugitive Slave Act. A fugitive was a slave who escaped.

Chapter 4

Many Northern people thought the law was wrong. Many Northern people thought slavery was wrong.

▲ Some Northern people said the law was wrong.

Why Was the Underground Railroad Important?

Many Northern people did not return the slaves. Many Northern people helped the slaves.

▲ **Northern abolitionists helped the slaves.**

Chapter 4

Some Southern people were angry with Northern people. Some Northern people were angry about slavery. Finally the Civil War started.

Why Was the Underground Railroad Important?

The Civil War was between the North and the South. The Civil War started in 1861. The Civil War ended in 1865. The North won the Civil War.

Then and Now

The United States had slavery before the Civil War. The United States ended slavery in 1865. Now, the United States does not have slavery.

▲ The Civil War started.

Summary

The Underground Railroad was a way to freedom. Slaves used the routes to escape the South. Abolitionists helped thousands of slaves to escape. Harriet Tubman was a conductor on the Underground Railroad. The Underground Railroad was very important.

The Underground Railroad

1770s–1865

The United States had slavery. Slaves wanted to be free.

1820

Harriet Tubman was born.

1830–1861

Slaves used the Underground Railroad to escape. Thousands of slaves escaped.

1849	1850	1861	1865
Harriet Tubman became a conductor on the Underground Railroad.	The Fugitive Slave Act became a law.	The Civil War started.	The Civil War ended.

▶ Think About It

1. What was the Underground Railroad?
2. Why were the abolitionists important?
3. Why was the Underground Railroad important?

Glossary

abolitionists people who thought slavery was wrong

Abolitionists helped the slaves to escape.

escape to get away

Tubman helped slaves to escape.

Harriet Tubman a famous abolitionist

Harriet Tubman showed many slaves the routes.

law a government rule

The law said the slaves must return.

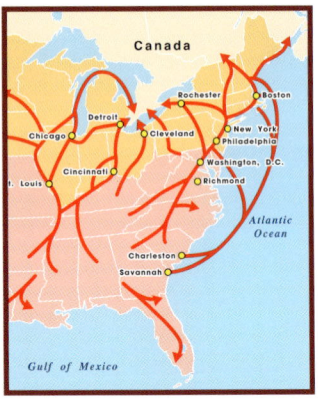

routes ways to follow

The Underground Railroad routes went from the South.

slavery people owning other people

The United States had slavery long ago.

slaves people owned by other people

*The **slaves** wanted to escape.*

the North the Northern states

*Some slaves lived in **the North**.*

the South the Southern states

*Most slaves lived in **the South**.*

Underground Railroad (1) routes slaves used to escape; (2) the people who helped slaves escape

*Slaves used the **Underground Railroad** to escape.*

Index

abolitionists, 11–12, 14–15, 18, 28

Africa, 4

African Americans, 15

cabins, 7

Canada, 9–10, 22

Civil War, 26–27

crops, 6

escape, 2, 9–11, 18, 20–22, 28

law, 23–24

Maryland, 19

Mexico, 9–10, 22

North Star, 13

North, the, 5, 9–10, 20, 22, 27

Pennsylvania, 20

plantations, 5–6

Quakers, 15

routes, 10, 12, 21, 28

slavery, 2–4, 11, 24, 26

slaves, 2, 4–14, 18, 21–23, 25, 28

South, the, 5, 9–10, 23, 27

Tubman, Harriet, 18–21, 28

Underground Railroad, 2–3, 10–11, 16, 18, 20–22, 28

United States, 2, 4